To *Sophie*

Enjoy your visit to the beautiful Philippines through a journey with this book. My wish is for you to learn about the wonderful people, animals, foods and more.

Love, *Grandma*

A note to you, dear *reader,*

The Philippines is known for its many islands. It is also a land of many cultures, the earliest of which were in existence over 45,000 years ago! This was followed over time by many who have come from other nearby areas, especially Asia. Europeans also influenced Filipino culture in more recent colonial years. This all results in the rich blend of ancestry and modern culture of food, language, music, sports and more! This book is a visit to recent times, realizing and respecting the original peoples whose children lived and laughed there so long ago. My hope is the children to whom you read this book can learn this respect for and love of people and cultures around the world, whether this is their own heritage or one they are embracing through this story.

Hello! Kumusta po kayo!

My name is *Sophie.*

This is my friend Panda Buddy. We are visiting the Philippines, a country made up of over 7,600 islands in Southeast Asia! There are more than 120 languages, though English and Filipino are the official languages.

Watch for Panda Buddy hiding throughout the story! There is also a Philippine flag in the book. See if you can find it! Hint: The main colours are blue and red, and there is a yellow sun and three little stars!

THE PHILIPPINES

Here is the Philippines, in Southeast Asia. The South China Sea is on the west side of the many Philippine Islands, and the Pacific Ocean is on the east side. The many islands are part of three island groups, so we will stop by each one. You can look at the map at the end of our journey to see all the places about which we visit and learn!

We've landed in Manila! I'm ready to run
Through the beautiful parks and more.
There's even a children's museum.
Let's see what we have in store!

This amazing park is still referred to as Luneta, but the name changed to Rizal Park long ago. Many cultural festivals are held here. A number of the country's festivals are connected to Catholic traditions.
Rizal Park
Open Air
Auditorium

Let's sing along to a band at Luneta Park
Can you find three tigers at the zoo?
Let's explore the Walled City, going back in time!
There's so much for us to do!

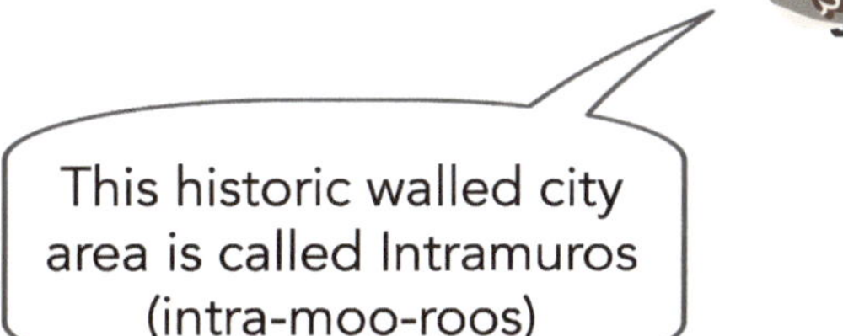

Peanuts and mangoes
are big crops grown in
the Philippines.
They also grow a lot
of bananas!
Bananas cue are deep
fried and coated with
brown sugar.

We are munching on peanuts and fried bananas too
On the Baywalk by Manila Bay.
There used to be Nilad bushes that gave
The name "Manila" to this city, they say!

Find all the places we've been to.
Manila was great to explore.
Wave goodbye and head north to the country
To see and do even more!

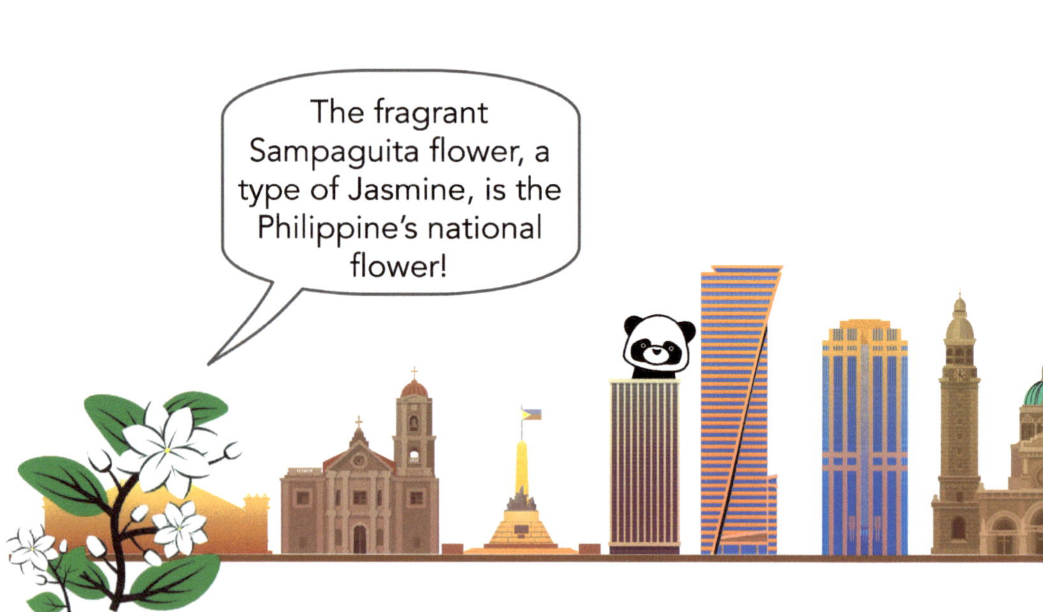

Kumusta!" greets the driver, "Hello, hop aboard!"
"I'll take you down to the stream."
Look around at the flowers and birds here.
It's so beautiful in the Philippines!

The Philippine Maya bird is well-known. It is also known as the Eurasian tree sparrow. There's even a folk song about this well-loved bird!

"Kumusta!" (koo-moos-ta): "How are you!"

Bump, bump, bump goes the jeepney, with colours so fun.
Over winding roads…Hold on!
There's a farmer ahead guiding carabaos.
Let's hop off at the stop just beyond.

The farmer waves back now to thank us.
Let's count carabaos: one, two, three…
Off drives the jeepney, finally reaching the end.
Now let's find out what we can see!

Look down by the river. There are shapes in the water.
The Philippine crocodile! Oh my!
And a dugong so peacefully gliding,
With a flick of his tail going by.

We drive to Tito Juan in the country. (tee-to Huwan)
I greet with a blessing "Mano po!"
And we are off now on an adventure.
I'll ride high on Tito's carabao!

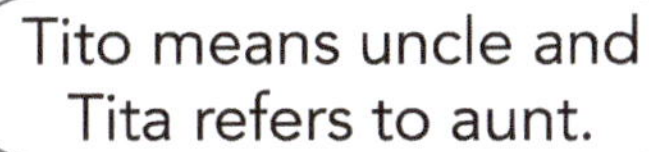

We are done our explorig. We are hungry!
Tito Juan and Tita Maria say: "Stay!"
I can't wait to taste all the food here,
After thank you, "Salamat po!" I say.

16

My tummy is full of chicken adobo
And tasty broiled milkfish to try.
Now I'm gobbling layers of cool halo-halo,
And ube cake, oh my!

Off we zip again. Wow things look different
Up at Baguio City, so cool.
They call it the Summer Capital here.
See? The mountain lakes sparkle like jewels!

We're playing Luksong baka, like a game of leapfrog
Now it looks like we are starting to prance.
The bamboo poles clap while we hop and jump
To the Tinikling traditional dance.

We're flying south now to see the Chocolate Hills!
Then bus to animals in the sanctuary.
Peer through dark. Watch the tarsiers blink!
How big are their eyes? Very!

I'm a tarsier at the Philippine Tarsier Sanctuary! Can you find all three of us?

Fly to Davao City, over beautiful Mount Apo.
Then duck down! We're at the Centre for eagles.
Spread your arms like their massive wing size.
These endangered eagles are regal.

Mount Apo is the country's highest. Ancient tribes revered it, naming it "Apo," as a respected relative.
The Philippine Eagle Center is a sanctuary for the critically endangered national bird. It is also known as a monkey-eating eagle!

Back to Manila to fly home after such a great visit.
Look at all the places we've been!
We say thanks and "Paalam" as we leave
These islands called the Philippines!

24

Besides goodbye, or "paalam," she would say: "Maraming salamat po" (thanks a lot) and "paalam" (goodbye)

It is really hot in the Philippines, so Sophie tried many delicious cold drinks. Here's an easy one for you to make. There are also a lot of mangoes grown in the Philippines. Enjoy!

Mango Smoothie

WHAT YOU NEED
1 Philippine mango (Carabao mango)
½ cup milk or coconut milk (or any milk)
1 tablespoon of sugar or honey
1/2 cup ice

HOW TO MAKE IT
Peel the mango and cut off the big pit. Put all the ingredients in a blender, puree and serve!

LEGEND

1. Manila
2. Baguio (Luzon Countryside)
3. Chocolate Hills and the Tarsier Sanctuary
4. Mount Apo
5. Philippine Eagle Center

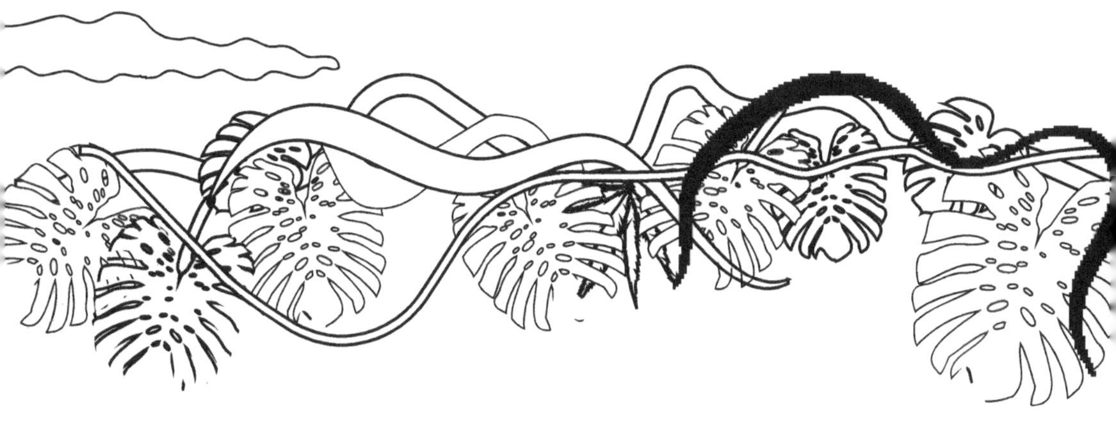

Here's your chance to colour!
You can look back in the book to
see these flowers, animals and
more from Sophie's travels in the
Philippines. You can colour them
the same, or use your imagination!
You can also colour Sophie
and Panda Buddy!

Candy

Candy loves kids' books, the sound of squeaky snow, and popcorn. She can't help reading books, especially if it lets her learn about people around the world. She read books to her little brother, then to her own kids, then to hundreds during her Library Programmer days. Now she reads to her grandkids. She even sends Grandma Videos to read to them from afar. Then, sometimes she just sits down and writes her own.

Jess

Jessica found her passion for drawing and designing at her grandparents house in Lima, Perú, where she would spend countless hours drawing and creating stories with her cousins. She loves art, reading, music, world history and culture, and animals of all kinds. Her two sons share her passion for animals and love to spoil their dog, Apollo.

Watch for other adventures as **Kids Visit the World.**

Guess what? Jacob is travelling across **Canada!**
And watch for more friends and places to come.

(Did you read **Isabelle Visits Perú?**)

@kids_visit_the_world

KidsVisitTheWorld@gmail.com

ISBN 978-0-9697032-2-8
Copyright @ 2024 - All rights reserved
Written by Candy Weisner
Designs by Jessica Ingard
Layout by J Bird Designs
Published by Thoughts For You
Made in Cochrane, Alberta, Canada

www.ingramcontent.com/pod-product-compliance
Lightning Source LLC
Chambersburg PA
CBHW041227050726
47599CB00001B/108